KIDS COLORING ADVENTURE

1 The Nature

Date:

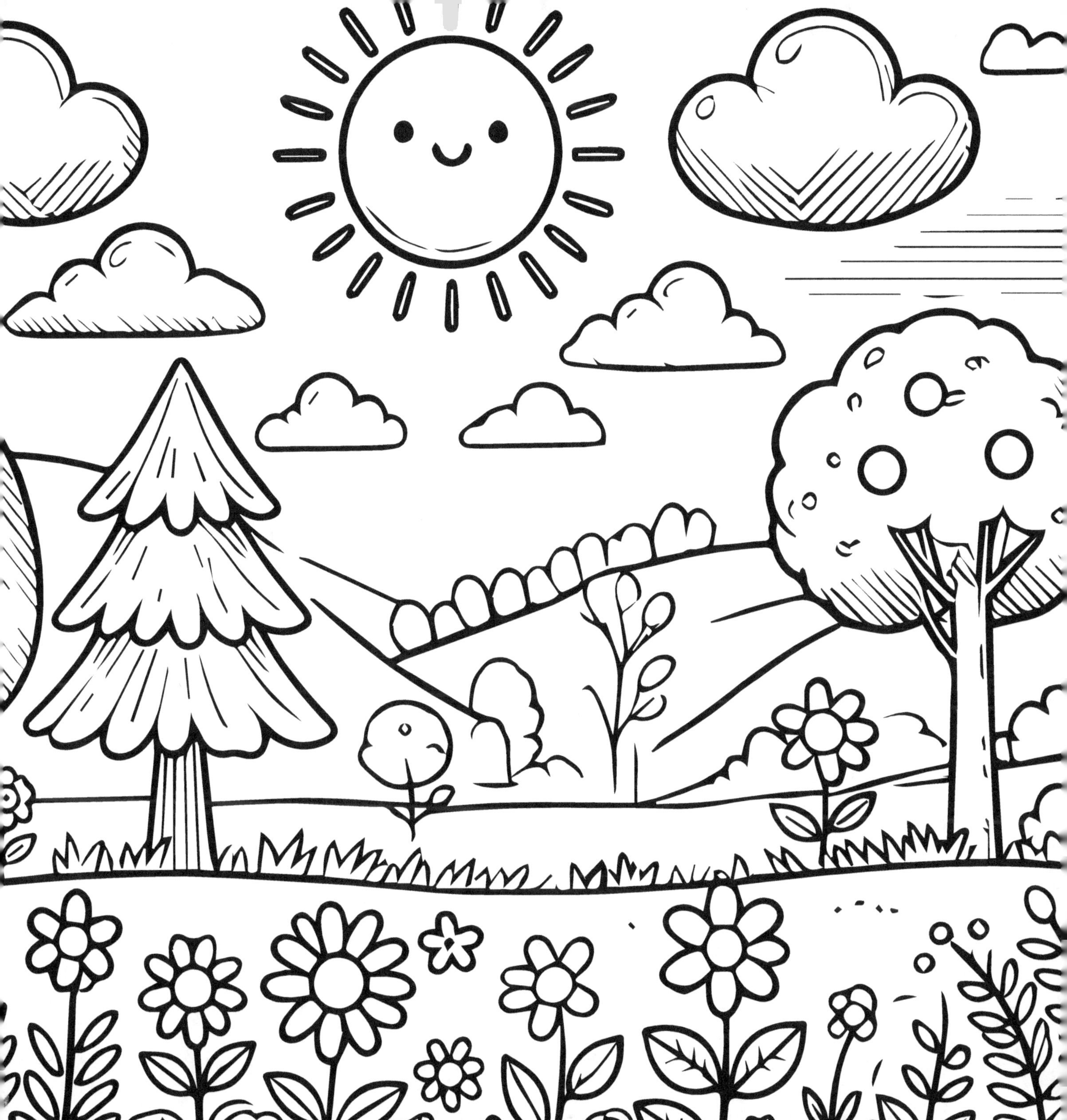

Date:

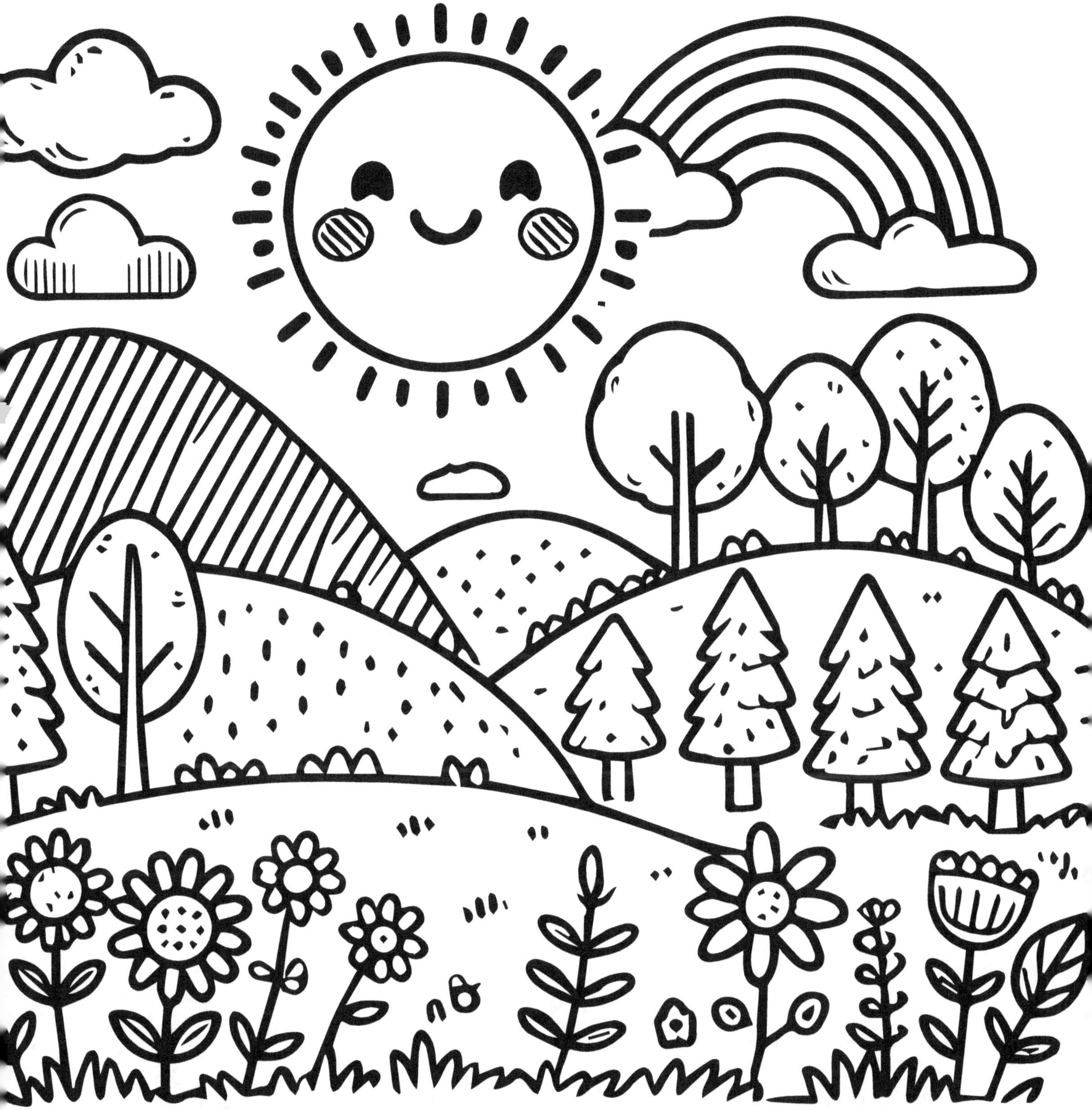

Date:

Date:

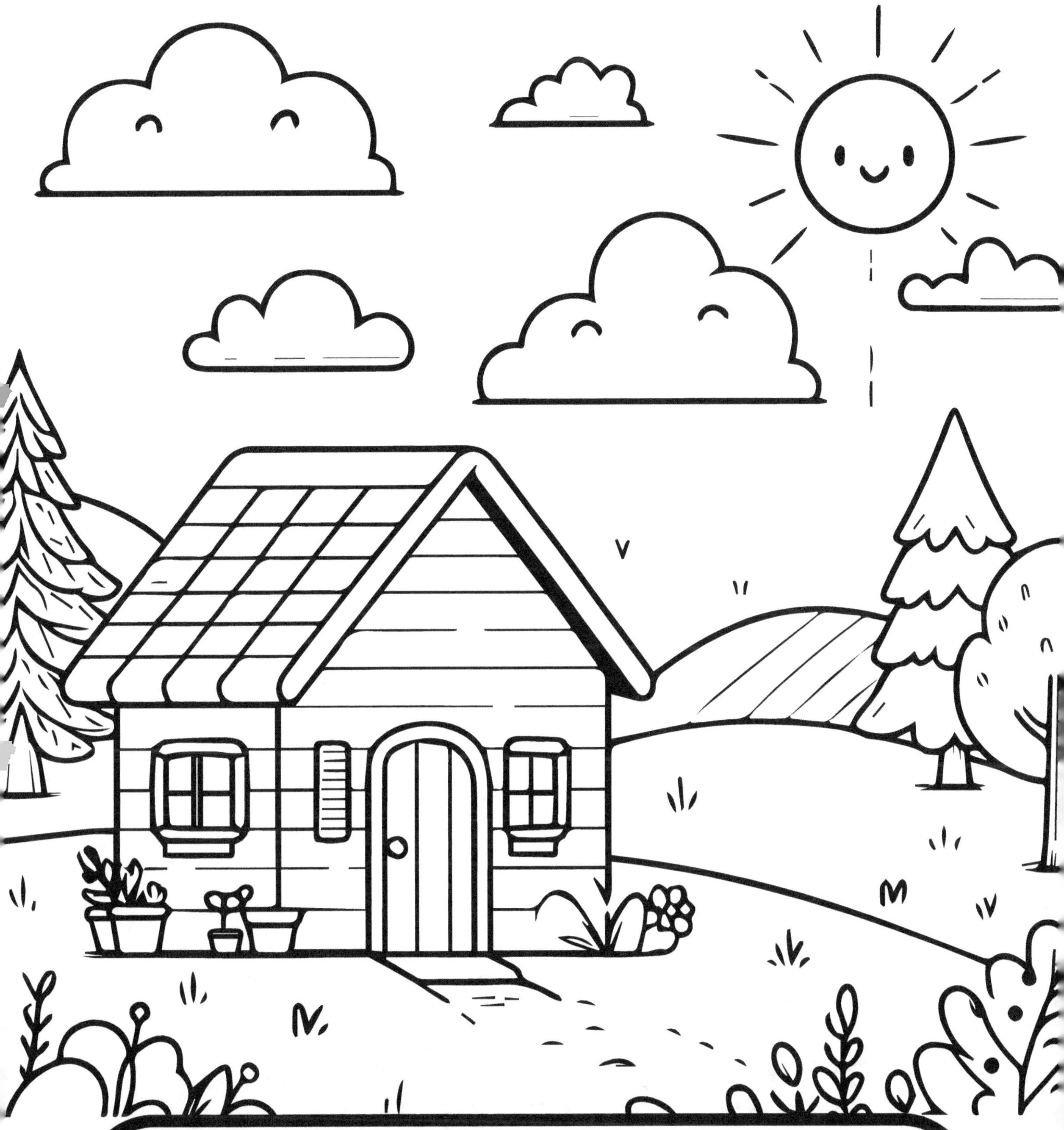

Date:

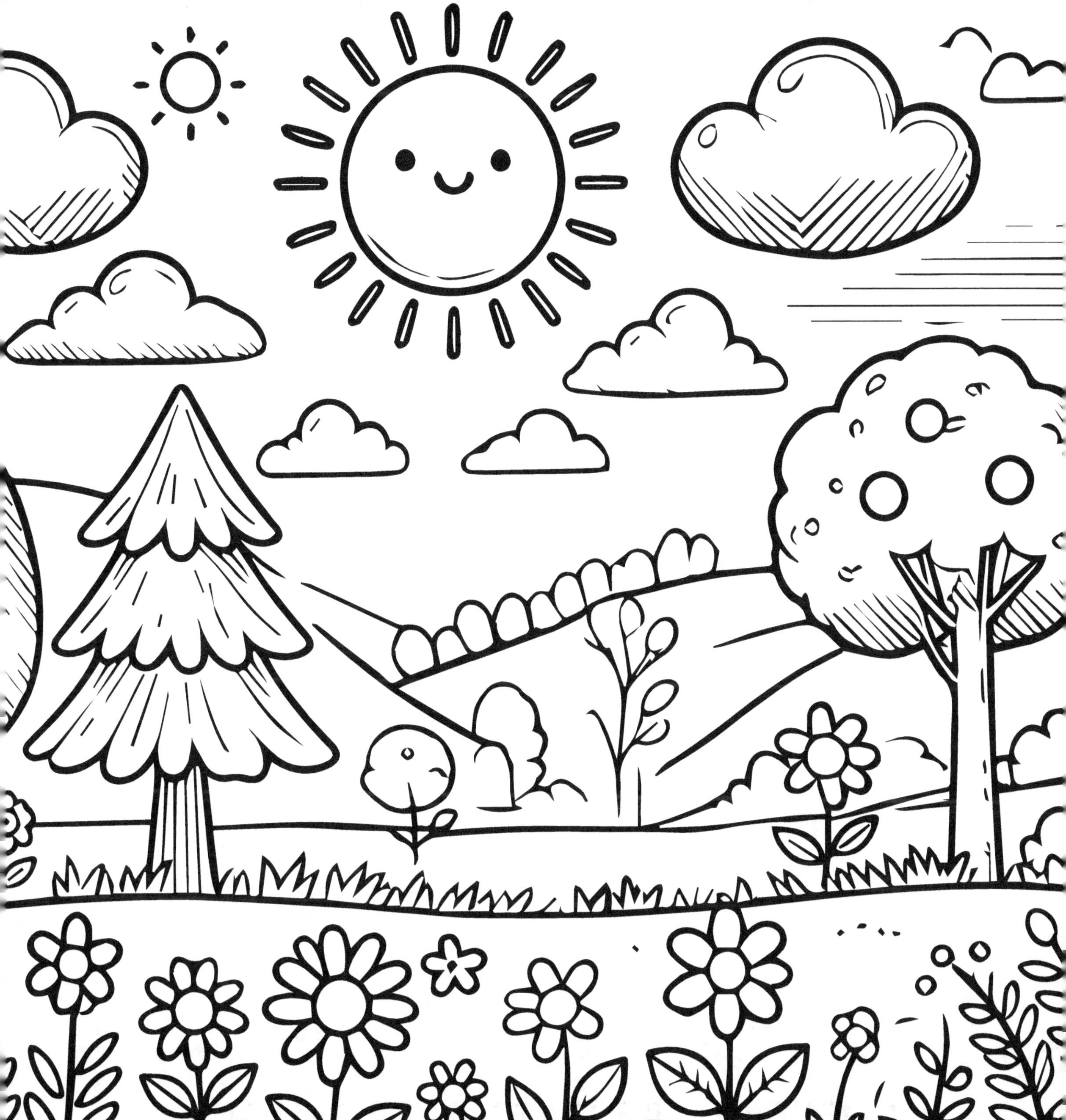

Date:

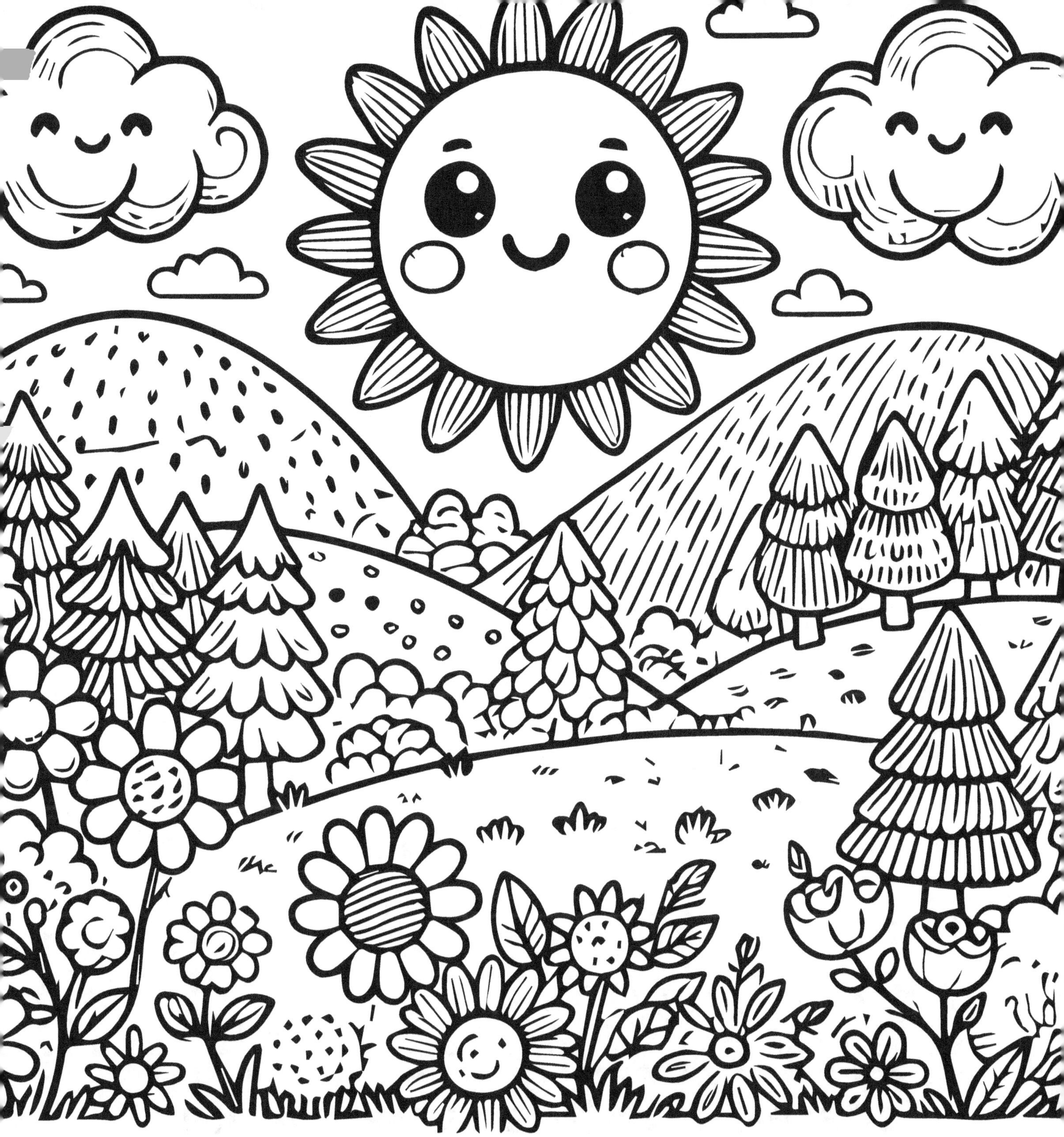

Date:

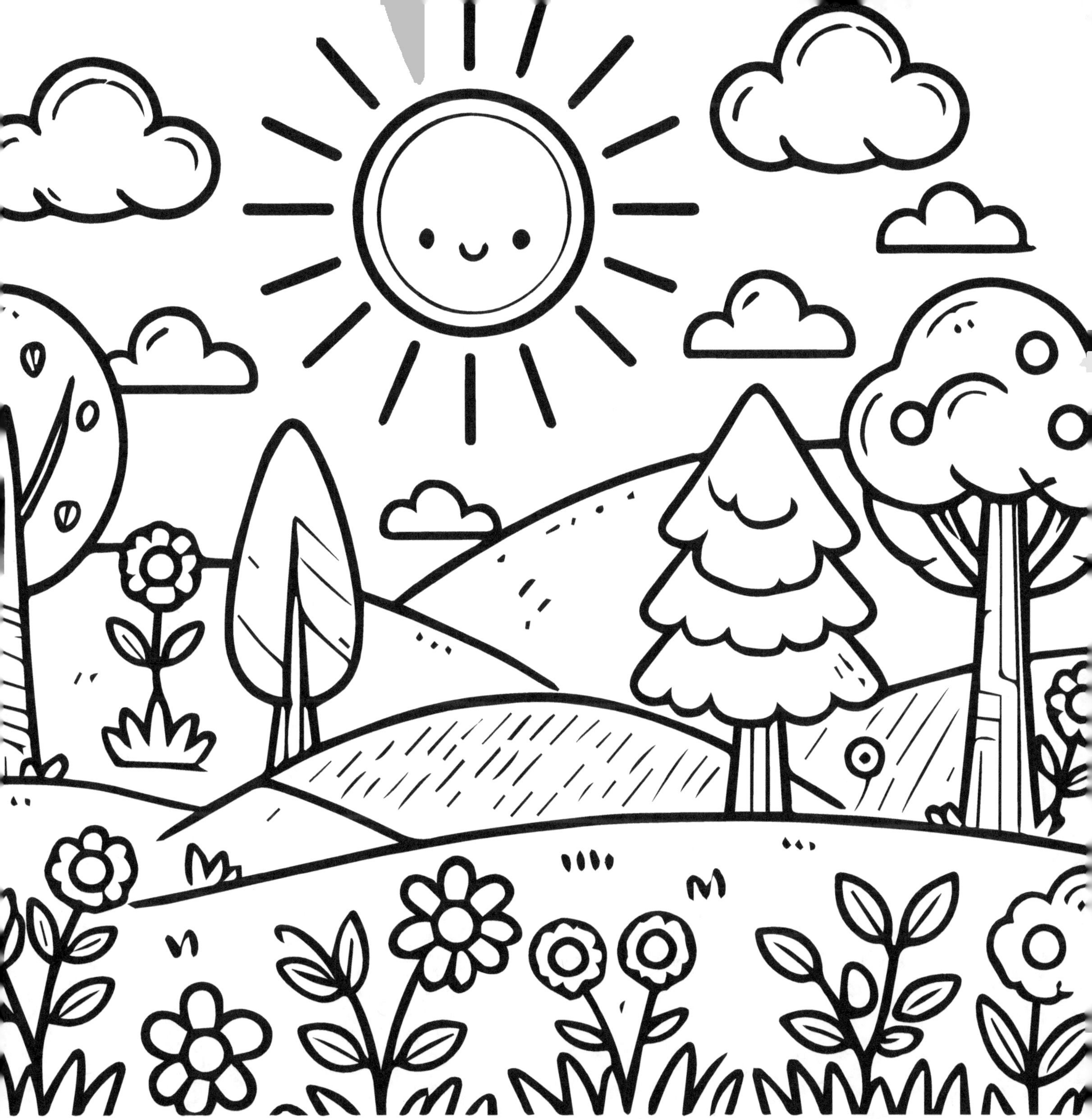

Date:

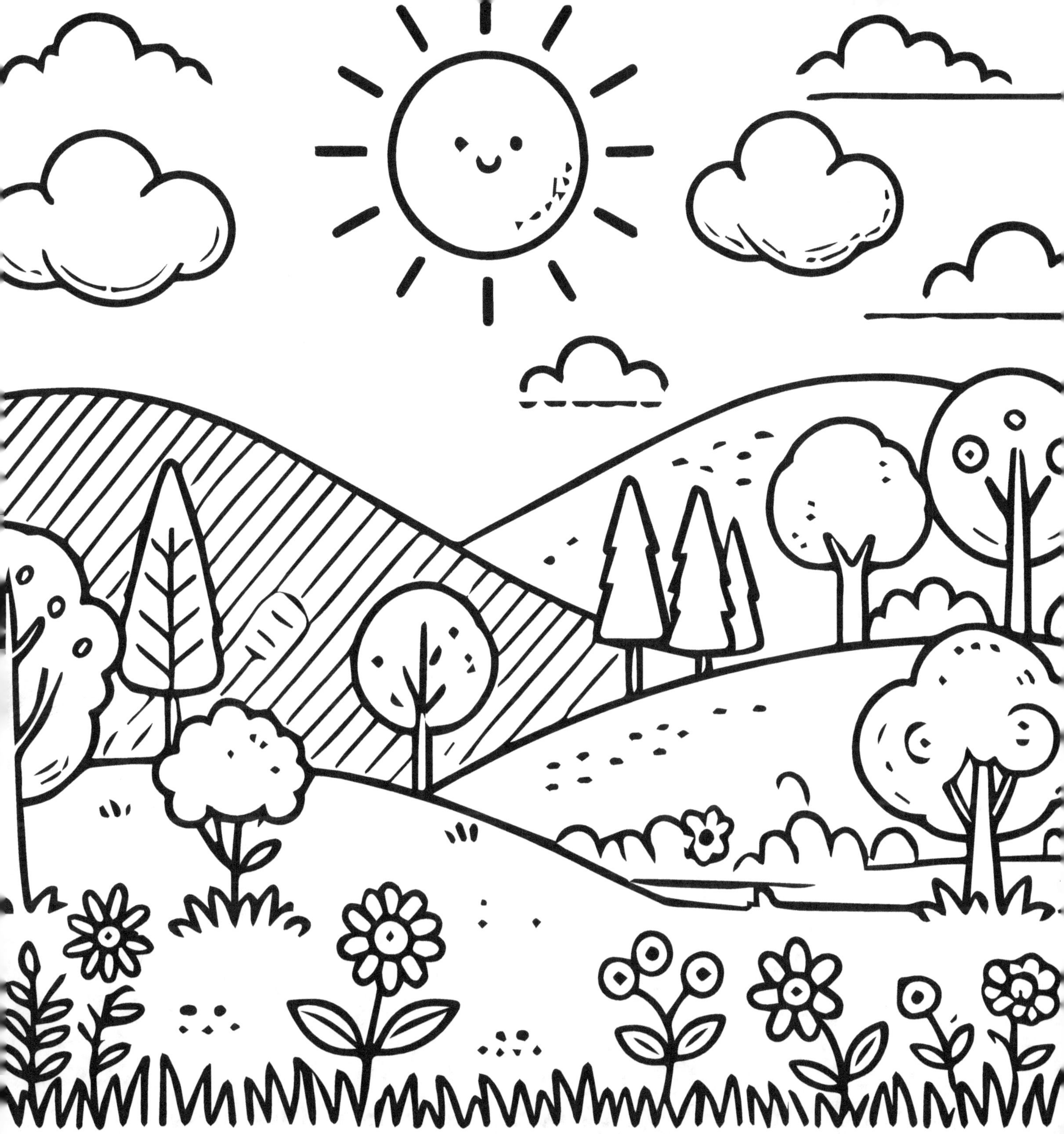

Date:

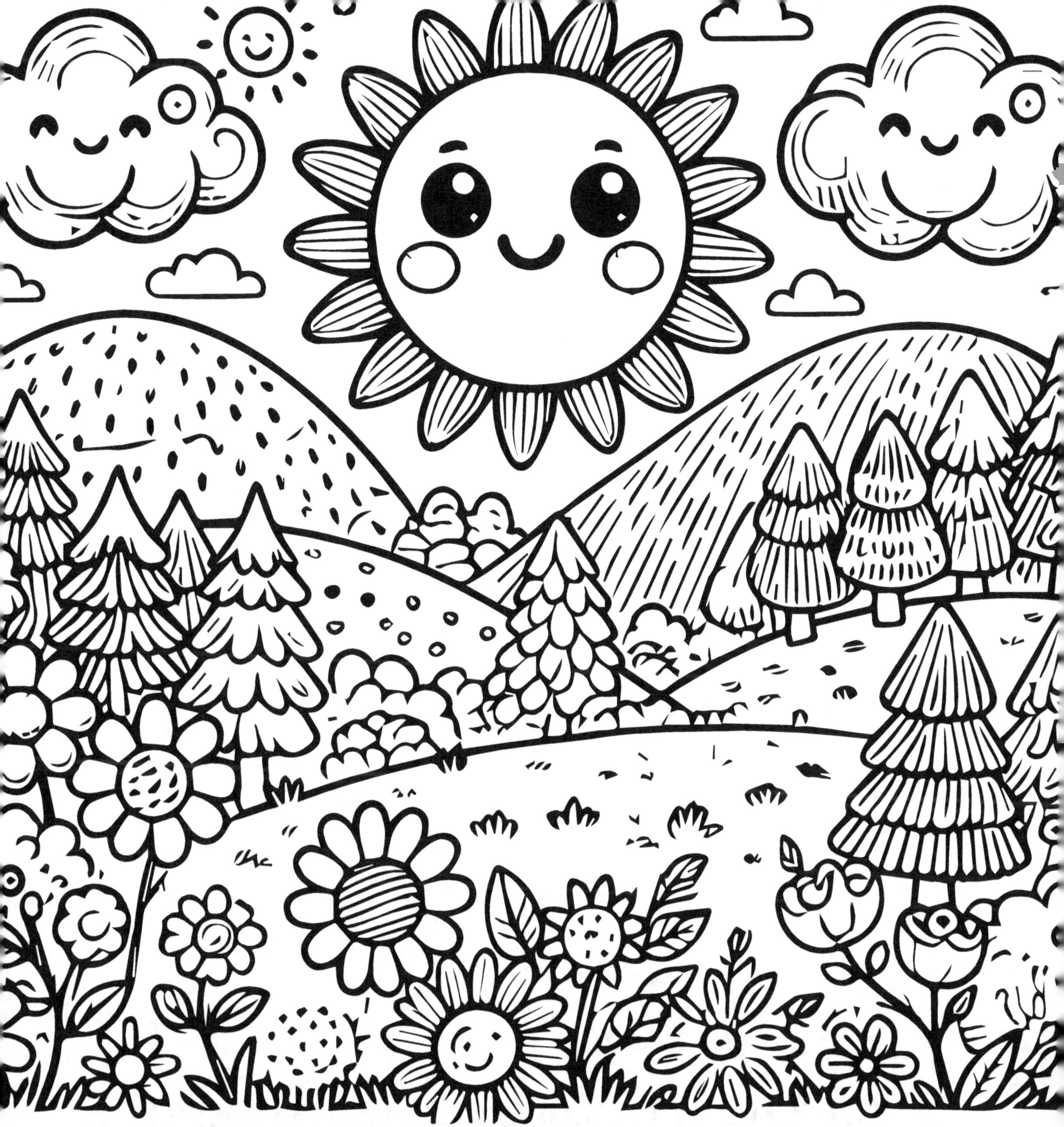

Date:

Date:

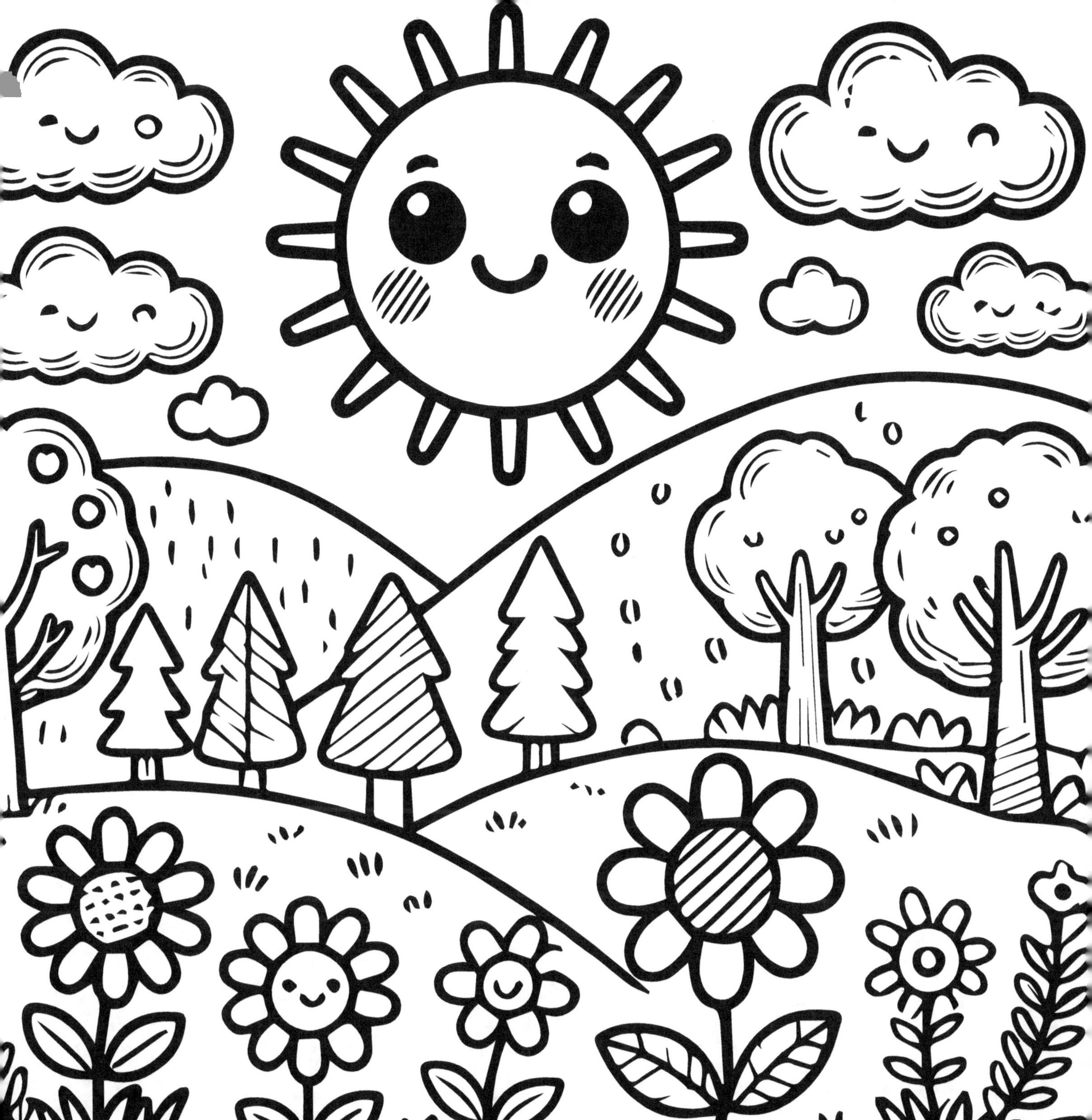

Date:

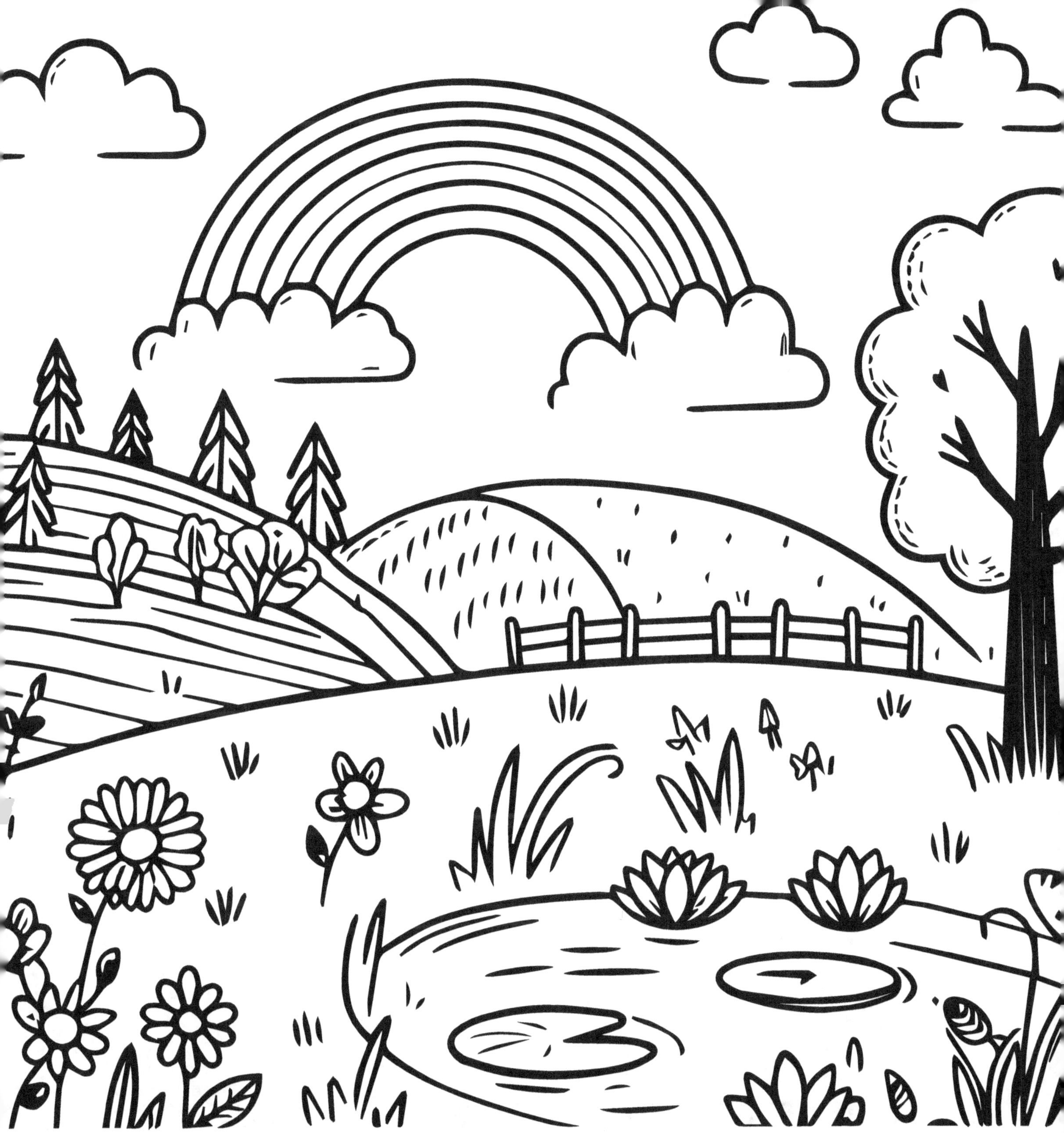

Date:

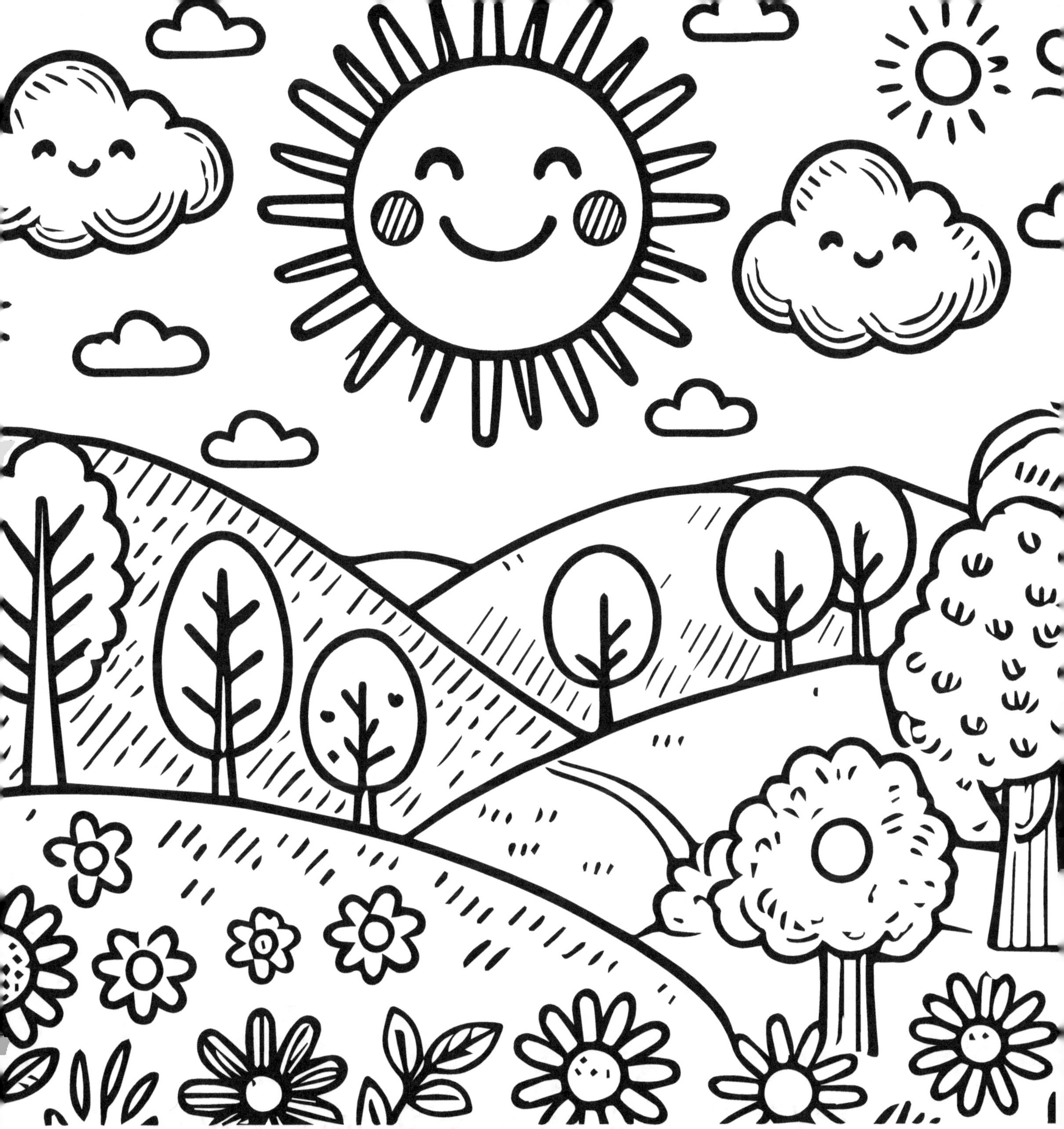

Date:

Date:

Date:

Date:

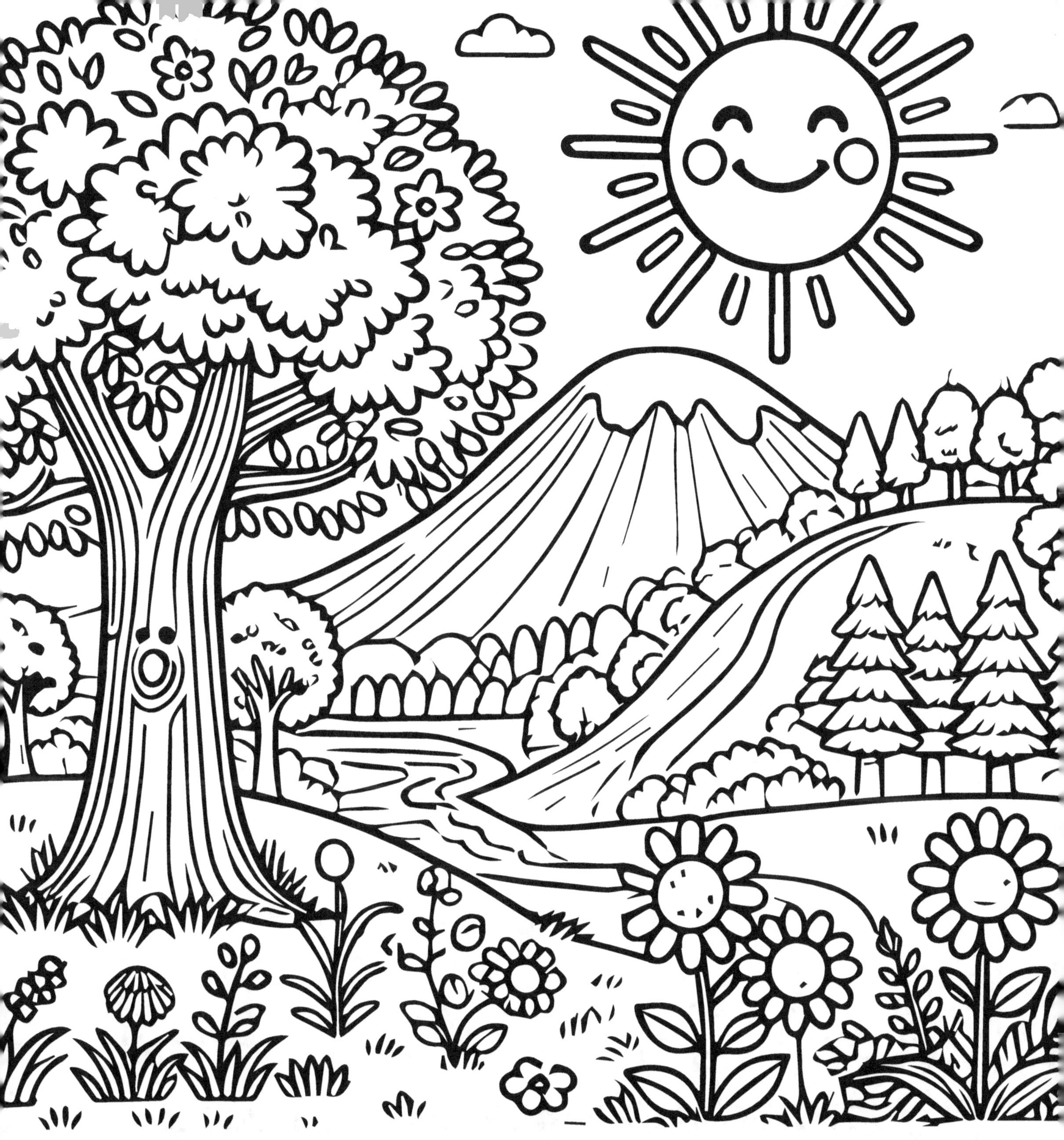

Date:

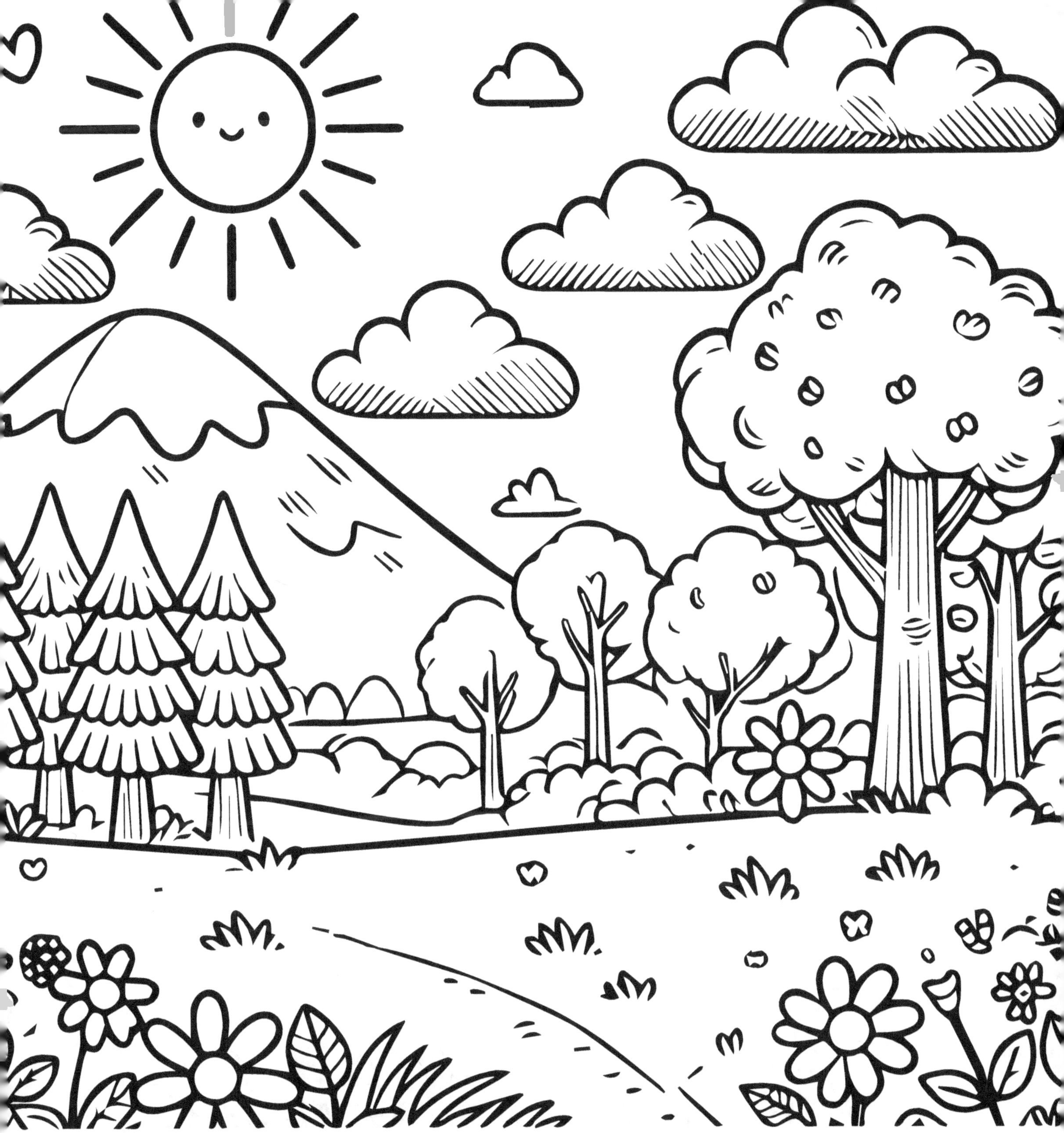

Date:

Date:

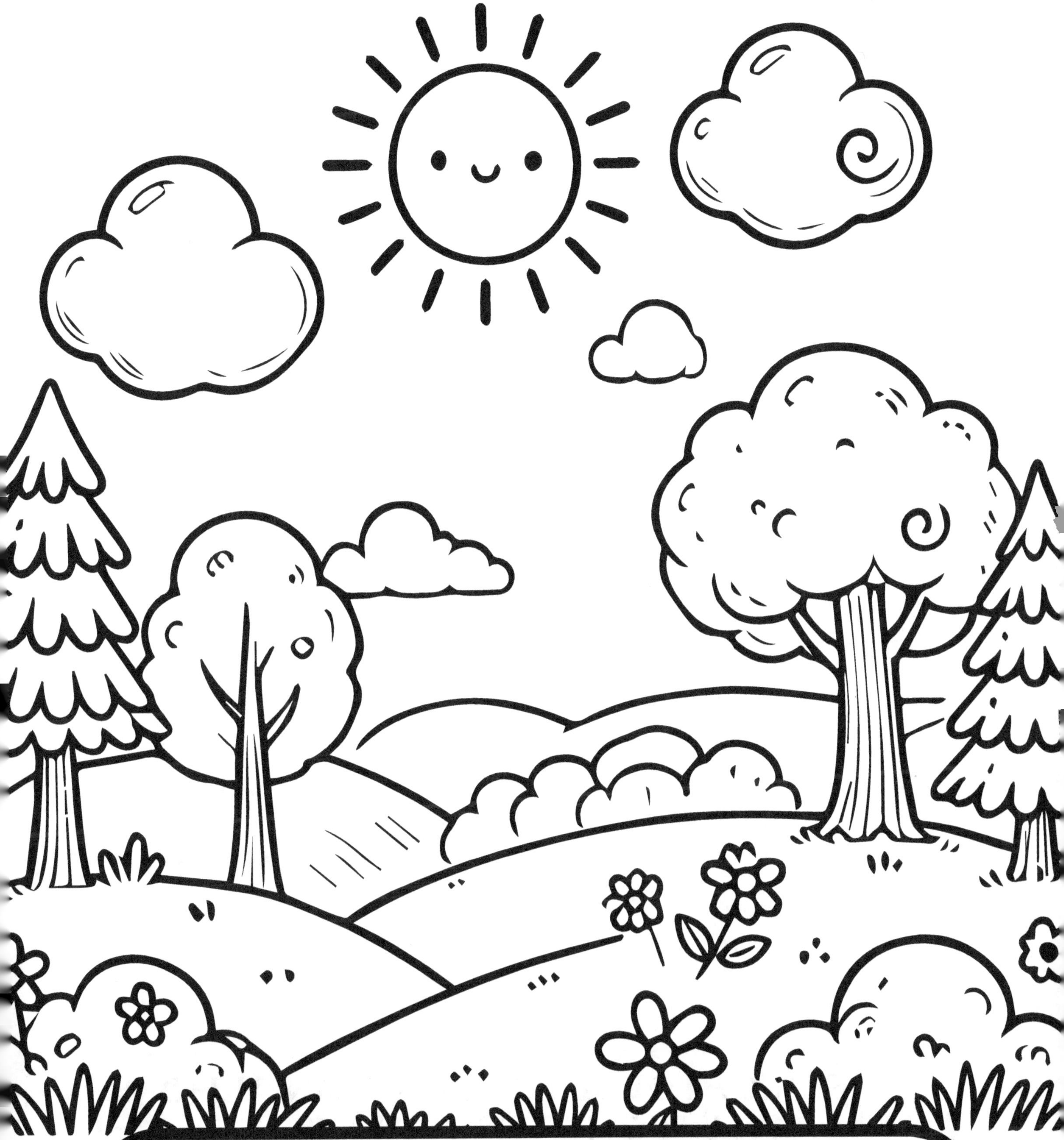

Date:

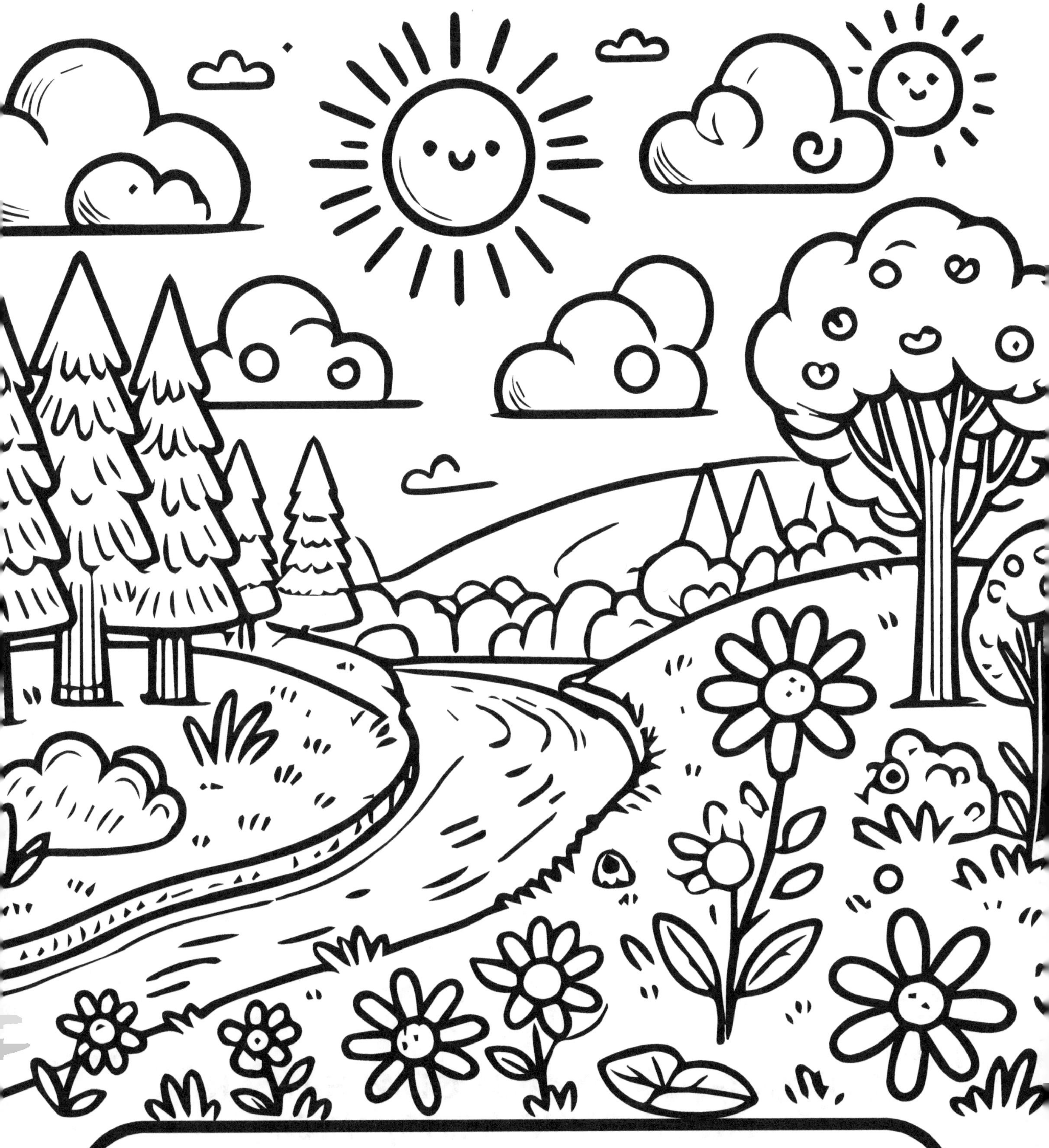

Date:

www.ingramcontent.com/pod-product-compliance
Lightning Source LLC
Chambersburg PA
CBHW081419220526
45467CB00009B/2746
9798389797451